Think Safety

I0482972

- More than 145,000 people work in over 7,000 warehouses.
- The fatal injury rate for the warehousing industry is higher than the national average for all industries.
- Potential hazards for workers in warehousing:
    - Unsafe use of forklifts;
    - Improper stacking of products;
    - Failure to use proper personal protective equipment;
    - Failure to follow proper lockout/tagout procedures;
    - Inadequate fire safety provisions; or
    - Repetitive motion injuries.

OSHA

**Occupational Safety and
Health Administration**
U.S. Department of Labor
www.osha.gov

Hazards & Solutions

Warehouse operations can present a wide variety of potential hazards for the worker.

For warehousing establishments, the 10 OSHA standards most frequently included in the agency's citations were:
1. Forklifts
2. Hazard communication
3. Electrical, wiring methods
4. Electrical, system design
5. Guarding floor & wall openings and holes
6. Exits
7. Mechanical power transmission
8. Respiratory protection
9. Lockout/tagout
10. Portable fire extinguishers

OSHA
Occupational Safety and
Health Administration

Docks

Hazard: Injuries happen here when forklifts run off the dock, products fall on employees or equipment strikes a person.

Solutions:

- Drive forklifts slowly on docks and dock plates;
- Secure dock plates and check to see if the plate can safely support the load;
- Keep clear of dock edges and never back up forklifts to the dock's edge;
- Provide visual warnings near dock edges;
- Prohibit "dock jumping" by employees;
- Make sure that dock ladders and stairs meet OSHA specifications.

OSHA
Occupational Safety and
Health Administration

Forklifts

Hazard: About 100 employees are killed and 95,000 injured every year while operating forklifts in all industries. Forklift turnovers account for a significant percentage of these fatalities.

Solutions:

- Train, evaluate and certify all operators to ensure that they can operate forklifts safely;
- Do not allow anyone under 18 years old to operate a forklift;
- Properly maintain haulage equipment, including tires;
- Before using a forklift, examine it for hazardous conditions which would make it unsafe to operate;
- Follow safe procedures for picking up, putting down and stacking loads;
- Drive safely, never exceeding 5 mph and slow down in congested areas or those with slippery surfaces;

- Ensure that the operator wears a seatbelt installed by the manufacturer;

- Never drive up to a person standing in front of a fixed object such as a wall or stacked materials;

- Prohibit stunt driving and horseplay;

- Do not handle loads that are heavier than the weight capacity of the forklift;

- Remove unsafe or defective trucks from service until the defect is properly repaired;

- Maintain sufficiently safe clearances for aisles and at loading docks or passages where forklifts are used;

- Ensure adequate ventilation either by opened doors/windows or using a ventilation system to provide enough fresh air to keep concentrations of noxious gases from engine exhaust below acceptable limits;

- Provide covers and/or guardrails to protect workers from the hazards of open pits, tanks, vats and ditches;

- Train employees on the hazards associated with the combustion byproducts of forklift operation, such as carbon monoxide.

OSHA
**Occupational Safety and
Health Administration**

Conveyors

Hazard: Workers can be injured when they are caught in pinch points or in the in-going nip points, are hit by falling products or develop musculoskeletal disorders associated with awkward postures or repetitive motions.

Solutions:

- Inspect conveyors regularly;
- Ensure that pinch points are adequately guarded;
- Develop ways of locking out conveyors and train employees in these procedures;
- Provide proper lighting and working surfaces in the area surrounding the conveyor.

Materials Storage

Hazard: Improperly stored materials may fall and injure workers.

Solutions:

- Stack loads evenly and straight;
- Place heavier loads on lower or middle shelves;
- Remove one object at a time from shelves;
- Keep aisles and passageways clear and in good repair.

Occupational Safety and Health Administration

Manual Lifting/Handling

Hazard: Back injuries may occur from improper lifting or overexertion.

Solutions:

- Provide general ergonomics training and task-specific training;

- Minimize the need for lifting by using good design and engineering techniques;

- Lift properly and get a coworker to help if a product is too heavy.

OSHA
Occupational Safety and
Health Administration

Hazard Communication

Hazard: Chemical burns are possible if spills of hazardous materials occur.

Solutions:

• Maintain a Material Safety Data Sheet (MSDS) for each chemical to which workers are exposed in the facility;

• Follow instructions on the MSDS for handling chemical products;

• Train employees on the risks of each chemical being stored;

• Provide spill cleanup kits in any area where chemicals are stored;

• Have a written spill control plan;

• Train employees to clean up spills, protect themselves and properly dispose of used materials;

• Provide proper personal protective equipment and enforce its use;

• Store all chemicals safely and securely;

• Store chemicals away from forklift traffic areas.

Charging Stations

Hazard: Fires and explosion risks are possible unless proper guidelines are followed.

Solutions:

- Prohibit smoking and open flames in and around charging stations;

- Provide adequate ventilation to disperse fumes from gassing batteries;

- Ensure that fire extinguishers are available and fully charged;

- Provide proper personal protective equipment such as rubber gloves and eye and face protection;

- Properly position forklifts and apply brakes before attempting to change or charge batteries; follow required procedures when refueling gas or propane fueled forklifts;

- Provide conveyors, overhead hoists or equivalent materials handling equipment for servicing batteries;

- Provide an eyewashing and safety shower facility for employees exposed to battery acids.

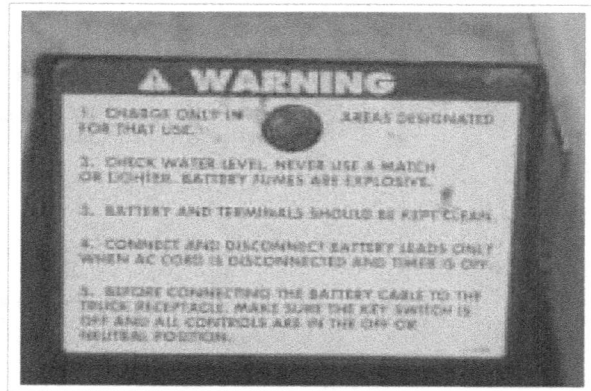

Poor Ergonomics

Hazard: Improper lifting, repetitive motion or poor design of operations can lead to musculoskeletal disorders in workers.

Solutions:

- If possible, use powered equipment instead of requiring a manual lift for heavy materials;
- Reduce lifts from shoulder height and from floor height by repositioning the shelf or bin;
- Ensure overhead lighting is adequate for the task at hand;
- Provide employees with task-oriented ergonomic training;
- Use your legs and keep your back in a natural position while lifting;
- Test the load to be lifted to estimate its weight, size and bulk, and to determine the proper lifting method;
- Get help if the load exceeds the maximum weight a person can lift safely without assistance;
- Don't twist while carrying a load, but shift your feet and take small steps in the direction you want to turn;
- Keep floors clean and free of slip and trip hazards.

OSHA
Occupational Safety and
Health Administration

Other Hazards

Inadequate fire safety provisions, improper use of lockout procedures and failure to wear personal protective equipment also create hazards in the warehouse workplace.

Employers should have an emergency plan that describes what is expected of employees in the event of an emergency, including:

- Provisions for emergency exit locations and evacuation procedures;

- Procedures for accounting for all employees and visitors;

- Location and use of fire extinguishers and other emergency equipment.

Warehouse operations need a lockout/tagout program to prevent equipment from being accidentally energized and injuring employees. Employees required to perform these operations should be trained and all employees should have a working knowledge of the program.

Finally, management at warehouse operations needs to conduct a site hazard assessment to determine what personal protective equipment (PPE) must be worn based on the hazards present and train warehouse employees on proper PPE selection, use and maintenance.

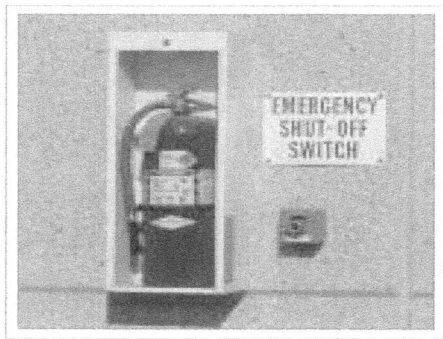

OSHA
Occupational Safety and
Health Administration

Think Safety Checklists

The following checklists may help you take steps to avoid hazards that cause injuries, illnesses and fatalities. As always, be cautious and seek help if you are concerned about a potential hazard.

General Safety

☐ Exposed or open loading dock doors and other areas that employees could fall 4 feet or more or walk off should be chained off, roped off or otherwise blocked.

☐ Floors and aisles are clear of clutter, electrical cords, hoses, spills and other hazards that could cause employees to slip, trip or fall.

☐ Proper work practices are factored into determining the time requirements for an employee to perform a task.

☐ Employees performing physical work have adequate periodic rest breaks to avoid fatigue levels that could result in greater risk of accidents and reduced quality of work.

☐ Newly-hired employees receive general ergonomics training and task-specific training.

☐ The warehouse is well ventilated.

☐ Employees are instructed on how to avoid heat stress in hot, humid environments.

☐ Employees are instructed on how to work in cold environments.

☐ The facility has lockout/tagout procedures.

OSHA
Occupational Safety and
Health Administration

Materials Handling Safety

☐ There are appropriately marked and sufficiently safe clearances for aisles and at loading docks or passageways where mechanical handling equipment is used.

☐ Loose/unboxed materials which might fall from a pile are properly stacked by blocking, interlocking or limiting the height of the pile to prevent falling hazards.

☐ Bags, containers, bundles, etc. are stored in tiers that are stacked, blocked, interlocked and limited in height so that they are stable and secure to prevent sliding or collapse.

☐ Storage areas are kept free from accumulation of materials that could lead to tripping, fire, explosion or pest infestations.

☐ Excessive vegetation is removed from building entrances, work or traffic areas to prevent possible trip or fall hazards due to visual obstructions.

☐ Derail and/or bumper blocks are provided on spur railroad tracks where a rolling car could contact other cars being worked on and at entrances to buildings, work or traffic areas.

☐ Covers and/or guardrails are provided to protect personnel from the hazards of stair openings in floors, meter or equipment pits and similar hazards.

☐ Personnel use proper lifting techniques.

☐ Elevators and hoists for lifting materials/ containers are properly used with adequate safe clearances, no obstructions, appropriate signals and directional warning signs.

OSHA
**Occupational Safety and
Health Administration**

Hazard Communication Safety

- [ ] All hazardous materials containers are properly labeled, indicating the chemical's identity, the manufacturer's name and address, and appropriate hazard warnings.

- [ ] There is an updated list of hazardous chemicals.

- [ ] The facility has a written program that covers hazard determination, including Material Safety Data Sheets (MSDSs), labeling and training.

- [ ] There is a system to check that each incoming chemical is accompanied by a MSDS.

- [ ] All employees are trained in the requirements of the hazard communication standard, the chemical hazards to which they are exposed, how to read and understand a MSDS and chemical labels, and on what precautions to take to prevent exposure.

- [ ] All employee training is documented.

- [ ] All outside contractors are given a complete list of chemical products, hazards and precautions.

- [ ] Procedures have been established to maintain and evaluate the effectiveness of the current program.

- [ ] Employees use proper personal protective equipment when handling chemicals.

- [ ] All chemicals are stored according to the manufacturer's recommendations and local or national fire codes.

Occupational Safety and Health Administration

Forklift Safety

☐ Powered industrial trucks (forklifts) meet the design and construction requirements established in American National Standard for Powered Industrial Trucks, Part II ANSI B56.1-1969.

☐ Written approval from the truck manufacturer has been obtained for any modifications or additions that affect the capacity and safe operation of the vehicle.

☐ Capacity, operation and maintenance instruction plates, tags or decals are changed to specify any modifications or additions to the vehicle.

☐ Nameplates and markings are in place and maintained in a legible condition.

☐ Forklifts that are used in hazardous locations are appropriately marked/approved for such use.

☐ Battery charging is conducted only in designated areas.

☐ Appropriate facilities are provided for flushing and neutralizing spilled electrolytes, for fire extinguishing, for protecting charging apparatus from damage by trucks and for adequate ventilation to disperse fumes from gassing batteries.

☐ Conveyors, overhead hoists or equivalent materials handling equipment are provided for handling batteries.

☐ Reinstalled batteries are properly positioned and secured.

☐ Carboy tilters or siphons are used for handling electrolytes.

OSHA
Occupational Safety and
Health Administration

☐ Forklifts are properly positioned and brakes applied before workers start to change or charge batteries.

☐ Vent caps are properly functioning.

☐ Precautions are taken to prevent smoking, open flames, sparks or electric arcs in battery charging areas and during storage/changing of propane fuel tanks.

☐ Tools and other metallic objects are kept away from the top of uncovered batteries.

☐ Concentrations of noxious gases and fumes are kept below acceptable levels.

☐ Forklift operators are competent to operate a vehicle safely as demonstrated by successful completion of training and evaluation conducted and certified by persons with the knowledge, training and experience to train operators and evaluate their performance.

☐ The training program content includes all truck-related topics, workplace-related topics and the requirements of 29 CFR 1910.178 for safe truck operation.

☐ Refresher training and evaluation is conducted whenever an operator has been observed operating the vehicle in an unsafe manner or has been involved in an accident or a near-miss incident.

☐ Refresher training and evaluation is conducted whenever an operator is assigned to drive a different type of truck or whenever a condition in the workplace changes in a manner that could affect safe operation of the truck.

☐ Evaluations of each operator's performance are conducted at least once every three years.

OSHA
Occupational Safety and
Health Administration

☐ Load engaging means are fully lowered, with controls neutralized, power shut off and brakes set when a forklift is left unattended.

☐ Operators maintain a safe distance from the edge of ramps or platforms while using forklifts on any elevated dock, platform or freight car.

☐ There is sufficient headroom for the forklift and operator under overhead installations, lights, pipes, sprinkler systems, etc.

☐ Overhead guards are provided in good condition to protect forklift operators from falling objects.

☐ Operators observe all traffic regulations, including authorized plant speed limits.

☐ Drivers are required to look in the direction of and keep a clear view of the path of travel.

☐ Operators run their trucks at a speed that will permit the vehicle to stop in a safe manner.

☐ Dock boards (bridge plates) are properly secured when loading or unloading from dock to truck.

☐ Stunt driving and horseplay are prohibited.

☐ All loads are stable, safely arranged and fit within the rated capacity of the truck.

☐ Operators fill fuel tanks only when the engine is not running.

☐ Replacement parts of trucks are equivalent in terms of safety with those used in the original design.

☐ Trucks are examined for safety before being placed into service and unsafe or defective trucks are removed from service.

OSHA
Occupational Safety and
Health Administration

Warehouse Safety & Health Resources

Most resource materials can be found on the OSHA website: www.osha.gov

Materials Handling

Materials Handling and Storage
OSHA Publication 2236 (Revised 2002).
559KB PDF, 40 pages.
A comprehensive guide to hazards and safe work practices in handling materials.
http://www.osha.gov/Publications/osha2236.pdf

Electrical Hazards

Control of Hazardous Energy (Lockout/Tagout)
OSHA Publication 3120 (Revised 2002).
174 KB PDF, 45 pages.
This booklet presents OSHA's general requirements for controlling hazardous energy during service or maintenance of machines or equipment.
http://www.osha.gov/Publications/osha3120.pdf

Controlling Electrical Hazards
OSHA Publication 3075 (Revised 2002).
349KB PDF, 71 pages.
This publication provides an overview of basic electrical safety on the job.
http://www.osha.gov/Publications/osha3075.pdf

Safety and Health Topics: Lockout/Tagout
OSHA website index to information about lockout/tagout, including hazard recognition, compliance, standards and directives, Review Commission and Administrative Law Judge Decisions, standard interpretations and Compliance Letters, compliance assistance and training.
http://www.osha.gov/SLTC/controlhazardous energy/index.html

OSHA
Occupational Safety and
Health Administration

Evacuation Plans and Procedures

An eTool designed to help small, low-hazard service or retail businesses implement an emergency action plan and comply with OSHA's emergency standards.
http://www.osha.gov/SLTC/etools/evacuation/index.html

Fire Safety

Safety and Health Topics: Fire Safety

OSHA website index to information on fire safety.
http://www.osha.gov/SLTC/firesafety/index.html

Fire Safety Advisor

OSHA's Fire Safety Advisor is an interactive expert software. It will help explain and apply OSHA's Fire Safety-related standards. It can be used online or is available for download.
http://www.osha.gov/dts/osta/oshasoft/softfirex.html

Forklift Safety

Safety and Health Topics: Powered Industrial Trucks

OSHA website index links to specific requirements and other Federal agency requirements.
http://www.osha.gov/SLTC/poweredindustrial-trucks/index.html

Sample Daily Checklists for Powered Industrial Trucks
http://www.osha.gov/dcsp/ote/trng-materials/pit/daily_pit_checklist.html

Preventing Injuries and Deaths of Workers Who Work Near Forklifts

NIOSH Alert Pub. No. 2001-109 (June 2001).
This alert instructs workers in the steps they can take to protect themselves near forklifts. It is also available as a downloadable PDF document.
http://www.cdc.gov/niosh/2001-109.html

OSHA
Occupational Safety and
Health Administration

Protecting Young Workers: Prohibition Against Young Workers Operating Forklifts
OSHA Safety and Health Bulletin (2003), 4 pages. Available as a PDF document, 109 KB.
http://www.osha.gov/dts/shib/shib093003.html

Hazard Communication

OSHA's website index for resources on hazard communication.
http://www.osha.gov/SLTC/hazardcommunications/index.html

More Hazard Communication

Frequently Asked Questions for Hazard Communication. OSHA, 6 pages.
http://www.osha.gov/html/faq-hazcom.html

Hazard Communication Standard.
OSHA Fact Sheet (1993), 3 pages.
http://www.osha.gov/pls/oshaweb/owadisp.shw
_document?p_table=FACT_SHEETS&p_id=151

Hazard Communication Guidelines for Compliance. OSHA Publication 3111 (2000), 112 KB PDF, 33 pages.
This document aids employers in understanding the Hazard Communication standard and in implementing a hazard communication program.
http://www.osha.gov/Publications/osha3111.pdf

Chemical Hazard Communication. OSHA Publication 3084 (1998), 248 KB PDF, 31 pages.
This booklet answers several basic questions about chemical hazard communication.
http://www.osha.gov/Publications/osha3084.pdf

NIOSH Pocket Guide to Chemical Hazards.
Handy source of general industrial hygiene information on several hundred chemicals/ classes for workers, employers and occupational health professionals.
http://www.cdc.gov/niosh/npg/npg.html

OSHA
Occupational Safety and
Health Administration

Ergonomics

Safety and Health Topics: Ergonomics
OSHA website index to resources and publications on ergonomics.
http://www.osha.gov/SLTC/ergonomics/index.html

Grocery Warehousing – Ergonomics
An e-tool specific for warehousing operations in the grocery industry.
http://www.osha.gov/SLTC/etools/grocery warehousing/index.html

Personal Protective Equipment

Safety and Health Topics:
Personal Protective Equipment
OSHA's website index to hazard recognition, control and training related to personal protective equipment.
http://www.osha.gov/SLTC/personalprotective equipment/index.html

Personal Protective Equipment. OSHA Publication 3151 (2004), 695KB PDF, 44 pages. *Discusses equipment most commonly used for protection for the head, including eyes and face, and the torso, arms, hands and feet. The use of equipment to protect against life-threatening hazards is also discussed.*
http://www.osha.gov/Publications/OSHA3151/osha3151.html

OSHA
Occupational Safety and
Health Administration

Warehouse Industry
Cooperative Programs

Voluntary Protection Programs
An OSHA Cooperative Program

Voluntary Protection Programs

Numerous VPP worksites that OSHA recognizes for their excellent safety and health management systems deal with the hazards of warehousing and storage. These model worksites are willing to share their expertise and many are available to mentor other businesses. For further information on how VPP participants can help you, contact the VPP Manager in your OSHA Regional Office or the Voluntary Protection Programs Participants' Association, 7600-E Leesburg Pike, Suite 440, Falls Church, VA 22043, telephone (703) 761-1146.

An OSHA Cooperative Program

Alliance Program

Alliances enable organizations committed to workplace safety and health to collaborate with OSHA to prevent injuries and illnesses in the workplace. A number of Alliances have an impact on the warehousing industry, including the following:

Retail Industry Leaders Association
The OSHA Alliance with the Retail Industry Leaders Association (RILA) is focused on

OSHA
Occupational Safety and
Health Administration

sharing safety and health best practices and technical knowledge, including ergonomics in retail warehousing and distribution facilities.

Industrial Truck Association

The Industrial Truck Association (ITA) and OSHA also have an Alliance to promote the safe operation of powered industrial trucks through training and outreach. The goal of the Alliance is to assist employers and employees in reducing and preventing exposure to potential hazards associated with the use of powered industrial trucks in general, and in warehouses in particular.

International Warehouse Logistics Association

OSHA and the International Warehouse Logistics Association (IWLA) work together to protect employees' safety and health, including hard-to-reach youth workers. The Alliance addresses materials handling, forklift safety, hazard communication and other issues unique to the public warehouse industry.

National Lumber and Building Material Dealers Association

OSHA has an Alliance with the National Lumber and Building Material Dealers Association (NLBMDA) to increase overall safety awareness in that industry while specifically addressing recordkeeping issues, preventing forklift accidents and avoiding lifting strains.

OSHA
Occupational Safety and
Health Administration

NJ Warehouse Operation - A Success Story

OSHA recommendations result in immediate, high payoff for an East Coast warehouse operation.

Injury Reduction

Recently, a New Jersey warehouse operation had been averaging two back injuries a month. After adopting several OSHA recommendations for reducing ergonomic risk factors specific to their operations, the company reported zero back injuries.

Boosting Morale & Productivity

And there was another benefit from adopting OSHA's recommendations. According to the Marlton, NJ OSHA area office, company sources reported that both the morale and productivity of the company's 50 warehouse employees had subsequently increased.

Ongoing Help

As part of OSHA's ongoing efforts to do a better job in promoting workers' safety and health, the agency has developed a program to help identify certain industries that have exceptionally high injury rates. One of these industries is warehousing. By identifying these workplaces, OSHA is better able to assist businesses in reducing their high injury rates. Through the Site Specific Targeting Plan, OSHA performs a comprehensive evaluation of a workplace and, with the help of its technical experts, helps the employer develop a plan for improving its employees' safety and health.

OSHA
Occupational Safety and
Health Administration

Specific Recommendations

OSHA's recommendations were developed specifically for this New Jersey warehouse operation by OSHA's Salt Lake City Technical Support Center following an inspection of the 186,000 square foot facility under the agency's Site Specific Targeting Plan which included a comprehensive walkaround of the workplace and a review of its injury records.

Avoiding MSDs

OSHA compliance officers worked with experts at the Salt Lake City Center to tailor specific recommendations to address the potential ergonomic risk factors they observed. Specialists at Salt Lake City analyzed the warehouse's various operations and recommended 19 steps, known as "feasible controls," that the employer could take to help employees to avoid muscu-losketal disorders (MSDs).

Hazards Identified

Some of the hazards identified by OSHA included:

- Employees had to reach elevated and distant locations in storage shelves to access materials;

- Workers had to repeatedly bend to reach low-level locations at floor level to access materials;

- Employees were lifting and placing heavy boxes onto pallets placed on the floor;

- Employees were performing forceful finger tasks with their wrists in bent postures while pricing products at poorly designed workstations.

OSHA
**Occupational Safety and
Health Administration**

Feasible Controls

In OSHA's detailed evaluation, each hazard was carefully described, including photographs illustrating the task to help clearly show the hazard. For each hazard, OSHA specialists detailed several feasible controls. These were straightforward, easy-to-implement actions such as:

• Adjusting the height of shelves;

• Providing stools or ladders to employees;

• Reducing the depth of shelving;

• Raising loading heights;

• Evaluating the flow and volume of orders so faster-moving products are placed on easier-to-reach shelves.

Also, OSHA's evaluation report detailed a list of available resources, including on-site consultation visits, that the company could use in developing improved ways to prevent injuries.

The company adopted 13 of the 19 feasible controls that OSHA recommended. And the result, thus far, speaks for itself: a perfect zero for back injuries, improved productivity and higher employee morale.

OSHA
Occupational Safety and
Health Administration

OSHA

**Occupational Safety and
Health Administration**
U.S. Department of Labor
www.osha.gov

OSHA's role is to assure the safety and health of America's workers by setting and enforcing standards; providing training, outreach and education; establishing partnerships; and encouraging continual improvement in workplace safety and health.

This informational booklet provides a general overview of a particular topic related to OSHA standards. It does not alter or determine compliance responsibilities in OSHA standards or the *Occupational Safety and Health Act of 1970*. Because interpretations and enforcement policy may change over time, you should consult current OSHA administrative interpretations and decisions by the Occupational Safety and Health Review Commission and the Courts for additional guidance on OSHA compliance requirements.

This information is available to sensory impaired individuals upon request. Voice phone: (202) 693-1999; teletypewriter (TTY) number: (877) 889-5627.